The Wittenberg Project

The Old Latin School

Rev. David L. Mahsman

Copyright © 2015 Concordia Publishing House
3558 S. Jefferson Ave., St. Louis, MO 63118–3968
1-800-325-3040 • www.cph.org

All rights reserved. No part of this publication may be reproduced, stored in a retrieval system, or transmitted, in any form or by any means, electronic, mechanical, photocopying, recording, or otherwise, without the prior written permission of Concordia Publishing House.

Unless otherwise noted, photos are courtesy of Rev. Dr. Matthew C. Harrison, Erik M. Lunsford, Dr. Bruce G. Kintz, Rev. Paul T. McCain, and Rev. David L. Mahsman.

Photos on pp. 47–48 are copyright by Cornelia Kirsh. Used by permission.

Manufactured in China

2 3 4 5 6 7 8 9 10   24 23 22 21 20 19 18 17 16

Table of Contents

Preface	4
Map	6
Introduction	7
What Is "The Wittenberg Project"?	9
The Old Latin School	13
How It All Began	15
The Wittenberg Project Is Born	16
Renovations Begin	22
Richtfest	46
Renovations Continue	49
Renovation Surprises	72
Dedication	78
Conference on Confessional Leadership	88

The Wittenberg Project

Preface

What is the Lutheran Reformation? It has been interpreted in various ways through the centuries. Some have defined it as a heroic event led by an individual of great fortitude and resolve, throwing off the bondage of church and an outmoded culture. It has been viewed as a German national event, even the birth of nationalism. It has been viewed as a decisive moment when modern man, conscience freed, broke through the maze and haze of authority and suppression of the inherently free individual. Protestant liberals look to Martin Luther as the author of freedom from the authority of texts, be they Bible or Confession. At its core, the Lutheran Reformation was none of these things.

> All these attempts to explain the Reformation are abortive, not because they are insufficient, but because they are false. Despite the kernel of truth which they contain, they are misleading. They are necessarily misleading because they do not approach the Reformation from that point of view from which alone it can be understood—from the point of view of the reality of the church. (Hermann Sasse, *Here We Stand* [St. Louis: Concordia, 1966], 50)

The Reformation was a call to repentance. It was a call to restoration, not revolution. It was a movement to acknowledge the sole sufficient grace of God in Christ Jesus, apprehended by faith alone, and doled out in the Word of God preached, in Baptism, Absolution, and the Lord's Supper. Luther called the church to absolute dependence upon God in Christ's cross and to the sole authority of Holy Scripture for all matters of doctrine and life. The cry "Repent," first uttered by John the Baptist (Matthew 3), was repeated by Jesus Himself immediately following (Matthew 4). The first of the Ninety-five Theses states, "When our Lord and Master Jesus Christ says 'Repent,' He wills that the entire life of the Christian be one of repentance." Repentance recognizes that we are beggars who only receive; indeed faith itself is a gift. Only repentant faith lays hold of grace, which is all gift, and all gift in Christ alone. Repentance bows before the majesty of Christ and His blessed Word.

This faith—*sola fide, sola gratia, solus Christus, sola scriptura*—is anything but nostalgia. The faith of

the New Testament, the faith of Luther, lives today and is found most fully in orthodox Lutheranism. And The Wittenberg Project is anything but nostalgia. The long and winding road from purchase to dedication of this building is but a flash in the 500-year history of the Lutheran Reformation. This project is about a continual call to repentance for all of us, and a call to faith in the Christ of the Scriptures, so eloquently confessed in the Lutheran Confessions. That is why the building is also a church plant. That is why the Old Latin School shall be a hub of activity promoting the catholic and apostolic faith of the Lutheran Reformation. That is why the Missouri Synod and her confessional sister church in Germany (SELK) are partners in this extraordinary endeavor. That is why the building at the epicenter of historical Lutheranism will be a beehive of activity for advancing the faith.

At the eve of the 500th anniversary of the Reformation, the world will turn its eyes, if only for a moment, to Wittenberg. But the burgeoning Lutheran churches of the southern hemisphere will, with ever-increasing intensity, continue to look toward Wittenberg. As I've traveled the globe these past 15 years, I'm shocked at the rising interest in this Lutheran faith—this Christ of the Scriptures taken seriously—an interest predominantly and numerically in the southern hemisphere. The Old Latin School—built in 1564 by August, Duke of Saxony (the same August who funded the Book of Concord)—where for at least 250 years the old Lutheran faith was taught to boys, from its new inception will gather Lutherans from around the world as we all endeavor to come to greater clarity on the faith once delivered to the saints. The very opening week (May 2015) will, *Deo volente*, see a conference of some 120 confessionally oriented Lutheran leaders from around the world. And the building, its pastors and staff, will welcome university students, pastors, laypeople, and hundreds of thousands of tourists who visit Wittenberg yearly, with the Gospel of the free forgiveness of sins in Christ.

Many have worked on this effort. Many more have contributed, and none more than Dr. Bruce G. Kintz and Concordia Publishing House. We thank God for Rev. David Mahsman, Managing Director, who has been indefatigable. We thank God for the International Lutheran Society of Wittenberg and its capable board members, especially Chairman Rev. Michael Kumm and Bishop Hans-Jörg Voigt of the SELK. We thank God for Rich Robertson and the Lutheran Church Extension Fund, for their expertise and strong support. We thank God for David Bueltmann and David Rohe, who years ago saw an opportunity and made the dream begin. We thank God for Bob Claus, Wilhelm Torgerson, Ulrich Schroeder, Jobst Schoene, Mark Hofman, the Schroeders, and many, many others. Finally, *Bürgermeister* Eckhard Naumann of Wittenberg has been as summarily helpful as he has been patient and gracious.

May this beautiful book serve as a remembrance of God's graciousness these past 500 years. May we forever treasure in these last times the blessed Gospel of Christ, as it runs its ancient course ever anew through this effort. And may this message of grace come to those, from Wittenberg to the far reaches of the globe, who do not know Christ.

Pastor Matthew C. Harrison
Assistant Pastor, Village Lutheran, Ladue, Missouri
President, The Lutheran Church—Missouri Synod
Second last Sunday of the Church Year, AD 2014

Map

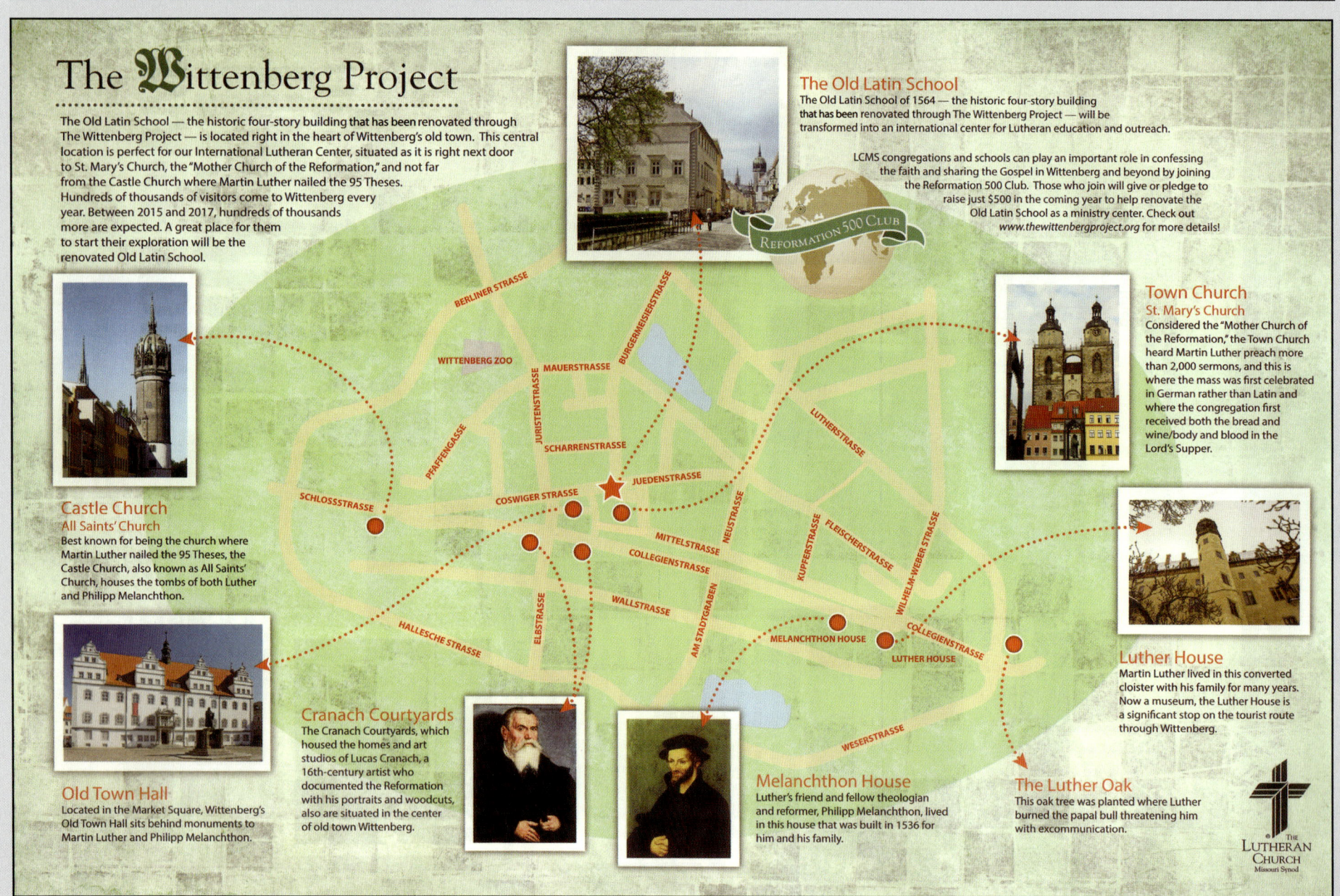

The Wittenberg Project

The Old Latin School — the historic four-story building that has been renovated through The Wittenberg Project — is located right in the heart of Wittenberg's old town. This central location is perfect for our International Lutheran Center, situated as it is right next door to St. Mary's Church, the "Mother Church of the Reformation," and not far from the Castle Church where Martin Luther nailed the 95 Theses. Hundreds of thousands of visitors come to Wittenberg every year. Between 2015 and 2017, hundreds of thousands more are expected. A great place for them to start their exploration will be the renovated Old Latin School.

The Old Latin School
The Old Latin School of 1564 — the historic four-story building that has been renovated through The Wittenberg Project — will be transformed into an international center for Lutheran education and outreach.

LCMS congregations and schools can play an important role in confessing the faith and sharing the Gospel in Wittenberg and beyond by joining the Reformation 500 Club. Those who join will give or pledge to raise just $500 in the coming year to help renovate the Old Latin School as a ministry center. Check out www.thewittenbergproject.org for more details!

Town Church
St. Mary's Church
Considered the "Mother Church of the Reformation," the Town Church heard Martin Luther preach more than 2,000 sermons, and this is where the mass was first celebrated in German rather than Latin and where the congregation first received both the bread and wine/body and blood in the Lord's Supper.

Castle Church
All Saints' Church
Best known for being the church where Martin Luther nailed the 95 Theses, the Castle Church, also known as All Saints' Church, houses the tombs of both Luther and Philipp Melanchthon.

Old Town Hall
Located in the Market Square, Wittenberg's Old Town Hall sits behind monuments to Martin Luther and Philipp Melanchthon.

Cranach Courtyards
The Cranach Courtyards, which housed the homes and art studios of Lucas Cranach, a 16th-century artist who documented the Reformation with his portraits and woodcuts, also are situated in the center of old town Wittenberg.

Melanchthon House
Luther's friend and fellow theologian and reformer, Philipp Melanchthon, lived in this house that was built in 1536 for him and his family.

Luther House
Martin Luther lived in this converted cloister with his family for many years. Now a museum, the Luther House is a significant stop on the tourist route through Wittenberg.

The Luther Oak
This oak tree was planted where Luther burned the papal bull threatening him with excommunication.

Introduction

God works through people.

Lutherstadt Wittenberg, Germany, is one of the world's special places. This is not simply because the town's history goes back more than 800 years, or because it's on the list of UNESCO (United Nations Educational, Scientific and Cultural Organization) World Heritage sites, or even because some very famous people once lived here. It's because God acted here in a particularly important way some 500 years ago, and as a result, we are immensely blessed still today.

Throughout all time, God has worked in and through various people to spread the Gospel of Jesus Christ, when and where He puts them in various callings and stations in life. At the time of the Reformation, God chose Martin Luther and his colleagues to help restore the centrality of the Gospel in the Church, a blessing we enjoy to this day.

It's because of Wittenberg's almost singular role in the history of salvation since apostolic times that there is a "Wittenberg Project" rather than a Berlin, Paris, or Rome project.

Illustration below:
Wittenberg, circa 1720. A city in the Electoral principality of Upper Saxony, famous for its university.

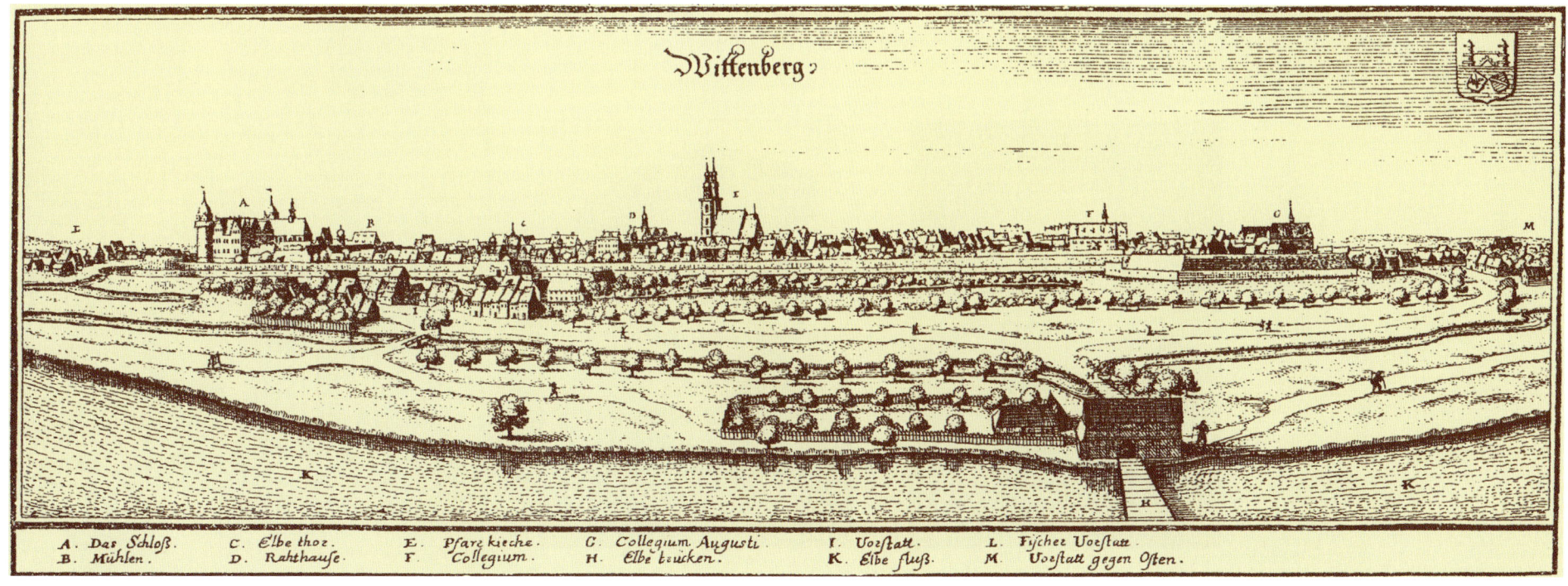

A. Das Schloß. C. Elbe thor. E. Pfarr kirche. G. Collegium Augusti. I. Vorstatt. L. Fischer Vorstatt.
B. Mühlen. D. Rathhause. F. Collegium. H. Elbe brucken. K. Elbe fluß. M. Vorstatt gegen Osten.

THE Wittenberg PROJECT

Prince Elector August I (1526–1586) was ruler of Saxony when construction began on the Old Latin School in 1564. (It wasn't the "old" Latin school then, of course, but something brand new.) His name is on the inscription above the *Kirchplatz* (church plaza) door of the school, along with those of the pastor and mayor. The elector's treasury funded a major part of the school building's construction costs with a grant of 350 Reichstaler. The total cost of the original building was just over 775 Reichstaler, so the elector provided nearly half the cost. (By way of comparison, the second largest contributor was Wittenberg University, which gave just over 52 Reichstaler.)

Elector August was a staunch defender of Luther's theology and was especially vigorous in his defense of the Lutheran understanding of the Lord's Supper over against those who were trying to introduce a more Calvinistic teaching in his land. August put his money where his mouth was, donating 70,000 Reichstaler toward preparation of the Book of Concord of 1580, which comprises our Lutheran Confessions and explains clearly the Lutheran understanding of Holy Scripture.

Left:
Prince Elector August I by Lucas Cranach the Younger.

Center:
Martin Luther by Workshop of Lucas Cranach the Elder (German, 1472–1553).

Right:
Martin Luther statue in the Wittenberg town square.

What is "The Wittenberg Project"?

In its very essence, **The Wittenberg Project** is Gospel ministry through Christian education and evangelistic outreach. It seeks to reach Christians and non-Christians, though in different ways and with different ends in mind.

The goal of the The Wittenberg Project is:

> To honor our Lutheran heritage as we approach the 500th anniversary of the Reformation by nurturing and strengthening the faith of Christians and introducing the Christian faith to non-Christians.

> Through development of a Christian education and outreach center in the very birthplace of the Reformation, we will attract students and visitors, promote confessional-Lutheran theology, and open doors to Gospel outreach and works of mercy.

The partners in this Gospel endeavor are The Lutheran Church—Missouri Synod, Concordia Publishing House, and Germany's Independent Evangelical-Lutheran Church (known as the SELK, short for its name in German, *Selbständige Evangelisch-Lutherische Kirche*). The three have established a German non-profit corporation, the International Lutheran Society of Wittenberg (ILSW), for the sake of doing ministry together in the town where Luther spent his entire career as a reformer.

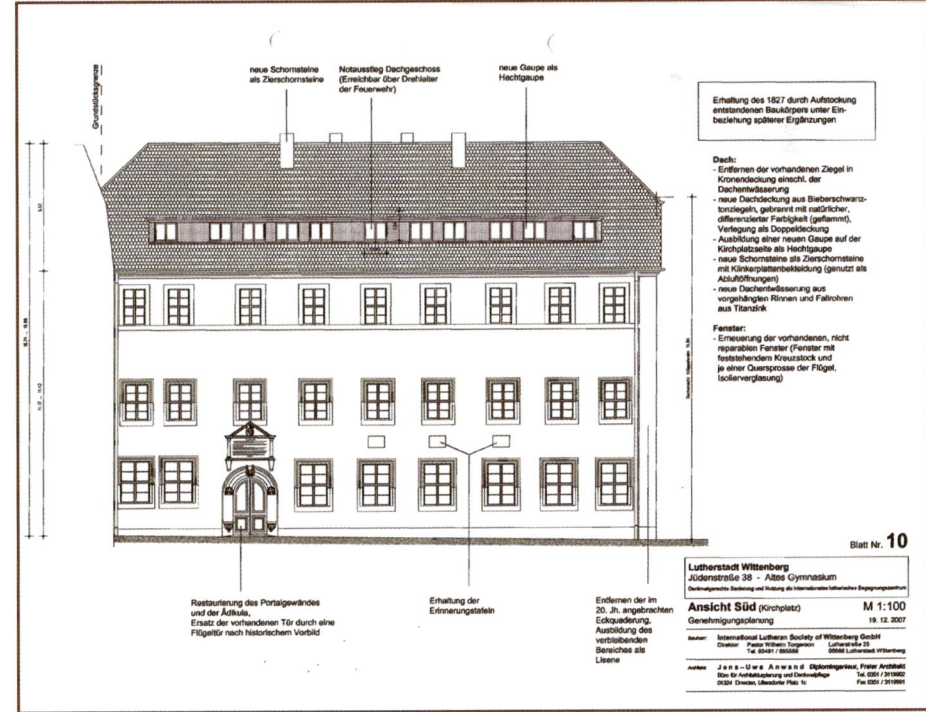

Top right:
  A view of the Old Latin School prior to renovation.

Bottom right:
  An early architect's drawing of the *Kirchplatz* side of the building.

It's understandable that many people think of The Wittenberg Project as an effort to renovate a historic building—the 450-year-old Old Latin School, or *Alte Lateinschule*—a phase of the project that is now completed. Buildings are concrete (no pun intended): they can be seen, touched, and photographed. This particular building is important; it's the place where ministry happens.

But it's the ministry that makes this so worthwhile.

Through the hard work of a committee of LCMS and SELK educators, we have developed—and continue to develop—programs that range from study-abroad opportunities for Lutheran university and seminary students to youth and elder hostel retreats and pilgrimages. We have even created a "confirmation capstone" immersion experience that will invite congregations to bring their confirmands to Wittenberg for a fuller understanding of their Lutheran heritage and their part in God's mission.

"If we manage to create an atmosphere in

Top left:
Real estate agent Eberhard Wattrodt, in tan jacket, shows the Old Latin School in 2006.

Top right:
Among those who met in June 2006 to lay the groundwork for The Wittenberg Project were (from left) Jonathan Schultz and Dr. Bruce G. Kintz of Concordia Publishing House; Rev. Dr. Wilhelm Torgerson, who proposed the project; and Rev. Dr. Robert Roegner, then executive director of the former LCMS Board for Mission Services.

Bottom right:
The Supervisory Board of the International Lutheran Society of Wittenberg (ILSW), guests, and LCMS Eurasia missionaries, who were meeting in Wittenberg at the time, gather at the Old Latin School for a photo in January 2013.

[the Old Latin School] that enables those who study there to have a keener understanding of their mission and to help them do mission, that part is a success," said Rev. Roger Zieger, director of SELK's Lutheran Church Mission and a member of the ILSW supervisory board. "It should be a place where the participants get a state of mind, a habit, that furthers the mission of God in the world."

The Wittenberg Project isn't just "continuing education" for Christians, however. It also provides us with a platform for Gospel outreach to those who visit Wittenberg and to the people who live in Wittenberg and the surrounding region. This may

Previous page, top:
Pioneers of The Wittenberg Project met together in June 2006. Among them, from left, were Dr. Bruce G. Kintz; Rev. Dr. Robert Rosin, who teaches Reformation history at Concordia Seminary, St. Louis; Jonathan Schultz; Rev. Roger Zieger, then the SELK superintendent (district president) for the area that includes Wittenberg; and Rev. Dr. Wilhelm Torgerson, then a member of the SELK *Kirchenleitung* (church council), who formally proposed the project.

Previous page, bottom:
LCMS President Rev. Dr. Matthew Harrison listens to a presentation at the January 2013 meeting of the ILSW Supervisory Board.

Bottom left:
Rev. David Mahsman, managing director of the ILSW, Dr. Bruce G. Kintz, and Bob Claus of St. Louis, who helped with raising funds for The Wittenberg Project, tour the construction site in January 2013.

Top right:
Rev. David Mahsman; Dr. Bruce G. Kintz; and Rev. Dr. Lawrence Rast, president of Concordia Theological Seminary, Fort Wayne, pay attention during an ILSW board meeting in January 2013.

Bottom right:
Participants in a January 2013 meeting of the ILSW board walk down Wittenberg's Juedenstrasse toward the Old Latin School.

be the place where the Reformation began, but today only about 15 to 18 percent of the people here profess to be Christian. Reaching the non-Christians with the Gospel isn't easy, but with God, nothing is impossible. One day, we hope to see a SELK congregation here where those who live in this place are fed the bread of life through Word and Sacrament.

The Old Latin School

God has provided us with an amazing location for the ministry in Lutherstadt Wittenberg. It's hard to imagine anything better.

The Old Latin School sits almost dead center in the heart of Lutherstadt Wittenberg's historic *Altstadt*, or old town. It dates to 1564 and is only about 35 yards, door to door, from the entrance to St. Mary's Church (the *Stadtkirche*, or Town Church), known as the "Mother Church of the Reformation."

The south door of the Old Latin School opens onto the *Kirchplatz* (church plaza) and faces St. Mary's, where Luther preached more than 2,000 sermons, where worship was once again in the language of the people, and where those partaking of the Lord's Supper finally received not only the bread and body of Christ but also the wine and His blood.

> By grace alone, through faith alone, on account of Christ alone.

Virtually every visitor to Wittenberg—up to 600,000 per year, with another 5,000 to 10,000 *per day* expected by 2017—makes a trip to the Town Church. That means they'll also be at our front door. This is our chance to offer hospitality, as well as information and presentations on the meaning and importance of the Reformation—that it's all about salvation by grace alone, through faith alone, on account of Christ alone.

And we don't have to try to explain to local folks how to find us. Our building is as familiar to them as the churches, the town hall, and the post office. They have known this building all their lives. The news media provided good coverage of the renovation work. And as an added bonus, a brand new regional shopping mall opened in late 2012 just across the street on the north side of our building. We had no idea when we bought the building that a magnet for those who live within 30 or more miles of town would be so

Above:
This sandstone plaque is above the door into the Old Latin School from the church plaza. In the triangle at the top is the electoral coat of arms. Written in Latin, the inscription shares Proverbs 27:11 and Colossians 2:2–3. Then follows:

"*In the Year of our Lord 1564, in the month of July, construction of the school was begun during the tenure of the most illustrious prince of Saxony, August, Elector in the Holy Roman Empire, who ruled this land and provided aid for the [school's] construction. Paul Eber, from Kitzingen, was the pastor of this church, and Thomas Heilinger was mayor of this city.*"

Top left:
   Real estate agent Eberhard Wattrodt unlocks the door in June 2006 to give The Wittenberg Project pioneers their first look ever at the Old Latin School.

Bottom left:
   Wood strips on the floor mark where walls will be located for dorm rooms in the Old Latin School.

Below top:
   Rev. David Mahsman, having arrived in Wittenberg in September 2009 as the new managing director of the ILSW, meets for the first time with the city's lord mayor, Eckhard Naumann.

close by the time we were ready to open our own doors.

Not only the location, but also the historic nature of the Old Latin School supports our ministry. This may well have been the first building anywhere in the world that was built specifically to be a Lutheran school. And while it's true that this was the *city* school, the city in 1564 was Lutheran, the students were Lutheran, the faculty was Lutheran, and the Lutheran pastor supervised it all—it *was* a Lutheran school.

We thank the Central Illinois District Church Extension Fund (CEF) for providing the funds from a bequest that allowed us to buy the building in the first place, and our donors for providing the means to make it into a place for so much ministry to happen and through which the Gospel can influence so many lives.

Left:
   Two of the original "founders" of The Wittenberg Project—Rev. Dr. Matthew Harrison, then executive director of LCMS World Relief/Human Care, and Rev. Dr. Robert Roegner, at the time executive director of LCMS World Mission—sit at the door of the Old Latin School.

How it all began

The initial idea that ultimately resulted in what we know today as The Wittenberg Project took root in 2004.

An international Lutheran theological conference was held that year in Lutherstadt Wittenberg. Among those present were the Rev. Dr. Wilhelm Torgerson, at the time pastor of a SELK congregation in Berlin and provost (a senior church official) for eastern Germany, and the Rev. Dr. Matthew Harrison, now LCMS president but then executive director of the Missouri Synod's former Board for Human Care Ministries.

"One day after lunch, we divided the participants into two groups for a walk through the city," Torgerson recalls. He led the tour for one of the groups.

"And one of my unforgettable memories is this incident: When we were in St. Mary's, I told them that this was Luther's preaching church, the Mother Church of the Reformation. One of the Russian brothers asked, 'So this is the Lutheran church in town?' And I had to respond, 'Well, it is a congregation of a union church, where both the Reformed and those calling themselves Lutheran claim to have a home.'

"And very similar at the Castle Church," Torgerson continues. "I pointed out Luther's grave, we had a prayer there, and upon being asked, 'Is *this* the Lutheran church?,' I again pointed out that it is a church of the EKD. And I noticed how some people just shook their heads."

EKD is the German abbreviation for the Evangelical Church of Germany, a federation of twenty regional Protestant churches that includes union as well as Lutheran and Reformed church bodies.

Torgerson and Harrison each credit the other with the idea for a confessional-Lutheran presence in Wittenberg. But regardless of who was the "instigator" (Torgerson's word), the idea for a joint project in Wittenberg soon began to take shape.

Bottom:
Rev. Dr. Wilhelm Torgerson, first managing director of the International Lutheran Society of Wittenberg, tells the history of the Castle Church to a tour group as they stand at Martin Luther's grave in the church.

The Wittenberg Project is Born

In 2005, Rev. Torgerson presented the idea to the SELK *Kirchenleitung*, the church council. He proposed working with the LCMS and reestablishing a SELK preaching station in Wittenberg; hosting the increasing number of visitors coming to Wittenberg; operating a "Lutheran Information and Reception Center" to foster inter-church discussions and theological conferences "in the realm of confessional Lutheranism"; and serving as a point of contact for other confessional-Lutheran churches internationally. The idea gained the SELK's approval.

Meanwhile, Rev. Dr. Matthew Harrison and Rev. Dr. Albert (Al) Collver were promoting the idea in the United States. An early partner was the Rev. Dr. Robert (Bob) Roegner, then executive director of the Missouri Synod's former Board for Mission Services (a.k.a. LCMS World Mission). They were soon joined by Rev. Paul T. McCain, who was acting president and CEO of Concordia Publishing House (CPH); Dr. Bruce G. Kintz, then vice president and chief operating officer (COO) of Concordia Publishing House, responsible for all finances and operations; and Jonathan Schultz, CPH corporate counsel.

In June 2006, Torgerson, Harrison, Roegner, McCain, Kintz, and Schultz met in Wittenberg to discuss the project and look at potential buildings. They were joined by SELK mission director Rev. Zieger, who is now a member of the ILSW board, and others,

Top left:
The tower of the Castle Church is a prominent landmark in Wittenberg.

Top right:
A sandstone plaque on the Juedenstrasse side of the Old Latin School commemorates the renovation and expansion of the building in 1828.

Bottom left:
Three presidents—Rev. Dr. Matthew C. Harrison (LCMS), Dr. Bruce G. Kintz (CPH), and Rev. Dr. Lawrence Rast (Concordia Theological Seminary, Fort Wayne), all members of the ILSW board—look around the Old Latin School construction site in January 2013.

Top:
SELK Bishop Hans-Jörg Voigt makes a point during the very first meeting of the ILSW Supervisory Board, in 2007.

Middle:
The Old Latin School *Dachgeschoss* (attic) after it was cleaned out in 2013 but before its renovation began.

Bottom:
A temporary resident in spring 2014.

including myself, at that time assistant to Rev. Roegner.

The three founders pledged financial support for up to five years through LCMS World Relief and Human Care, Concordia Publishing House, and LCMS World Mission. (It was not until 2009 that Wittenberg became a "church-to-church" project, rather than a project involving only the Human Care and World Mission units of the Synod.)

As we walked the streets of Luther's town, the idea of starting a project like this, in the birthplace of the Reformation, was exhilarating. So, already during this June 2006 visit, the group started looking at vacant buildings. And Wittenberg had plenty of those.

There's no question that the Old Latin School drew immediate attention. It was historic, it was relatively large, it was right in the center of the old town—and it was vacant. An immediate attempt to find the owner ensued. The search led to city hall, then to Wittenberg real estate agent Eberhard Wattrodt.

Wattrodt took the group through the building. The floors were littered with broken glass and fallen plaster. The only occupants for twenty years had been pigeons, who fouled the place considerably.

But excitement over the building was unabated.

"When Wattrodt said the building was owned by a bank," remembers Harrison, "I recall the energy leaving the discussion but saying, 'Call the bank!' He did."

"The bank was asking perhaps 200,000 euros for the building," Harrison says, adding that he believes it was Rev. Roegner who asked Wattrodt, "What would you give?" His answer was the euro equivalent of about $40,000.

"We looked at each other and said, 'OK, let's make the offer,'" Harrison recounts.

"Bob and I quickly headed to the airport in Berlin," Harrison continues. "I think we ended up hearing that the bank accepted our offer after we

Top left:
View of the Old Latin School entrance prior to renovation.

Bottom left:
LCMS President Matthew Harrison examines the third-floor ceiling as renovation gets under way.

Bottom center:
"Katie Luther" (tour guide Katja Köhler) explains the Wittenberg sites in an entertaining way to children.

Top right:
Visitors crowd the streets of old town Wittenberg on Reformation weekend every year.

Bottom right:
A view of the Old Latin School from the southeast prior to renovation.

Top photo, left to right:
Rev. Dr. Lawrence Rast; Rev. Dr. Michael Kumm, chairman of the ILSW Supervisory Board; and Dr. Bruce G. Kintz.

Bottom right:
Another view of the Old Latin School, this one from the northeast, before renovation began. The Castle Church is in the distance.

returned to the U.S. It so happened that the CEF folks in Central Illinois heard of our project, and a bequest recently received was offered to pay for the building. Perfect!"

By early 2007, the ILSW was established and Rev. Torgerson moved to Wittenberg to become its first managing director. (Torgy, as his friends call him, retired from that post in 2009, and I was appointed that same year by the ILSW board to succeed him.) In 2012, Rev. Michael Kumm became the board chairman of the ILSW. Through his leadership, the committee was kept on track and the project came to completion.

In the years that followed, the project had its share of fits and starts. Renovation plans for the old school were prepared, but sufficient funding for construction was not forthcoming. There was no unanimous support in either St. Louis or Hanover (headquarters of the SELK) for what the group had hoped to do in Wittenberg. And while the project's mission gained sharper focus, several different roads for getting there were tested and abandoned for one reason or another.

But that's water under the bridge. Since 2012, the project has made steady progress in its current direction as a Gospel-motivated and Gospel-based; distinctly Lutheran; Christian education, outreach, and welcome center in the renovated Old Latin School.

We are approaching 2017 and the 500th anniversary of the Reformation. This is an opportune time for us to act. Despite any changes in the details, The Wittenberg Project has always recognized Wittenberg's place in the history of salvation and, as a sign of gratitude for all that our Lord has done for us, has sought to serve and further God's mission in the world.

> "This is an opportune time for us to act."

Previous page:
The Wittenberg marketplace in 2010, with the towers of the Town Church in the center and the old Renaissance town hall to the left. The statues of Martin Luther and Philip Melanchthon had been removed for renovation.

Above:
Rain or shine, visitors to Wittenberg want to see the "Theses Door" of the Castle Church marking the spot where Martin Luther posted his Ninety-five Theses on October 31, 1517.

Left:
Above the Old Latin School door is the coat of arms of Wittenberg, which features the towers of the Town Church above the elector's coat of arms.

Below:
Another significant Wittenberg door is the *Kirchplatz* entrance to the Old Latin School.

Renovations begin

Far left:
In the box being lifted from the ground under the building's elevator are five skeletons—an adult and four children—discovered by state archaeologists. Archaeologists estimate the skeletons date from the thirteenth century, but further tests are required.

Top center:
Workers break up and remove the old floor on the first level of the building during the demolition phase of renovation.

Bottom center:
When floor boards were removed, workers discovered that the old wooden joists and beams were in far worse condition from rot and insect damage than initially expected.

Top right:
Construction supervisor Thomas Lübke (in hard hat) discusses next steps with Lutz Pade, who supervised the demolition phase of the renovation.

Below:
   Rebar was installed on the ground floor before new concrete was poured.

Center:
   A new wall is built in the foyer area of the ground floor.

Below:
   Right across the street from the Old Latin School, a new shopping mall was built in 2012, which should bring even more foot traffic and exposure to the building.

Clockwise, from top left:

    Although not in as bad a condition as the wood, many brick repairs also had to be made.

    The old stairway from the second floor to the third floor.

    The first section of scaffolding went up on the north side of the building in December 2013.

    Construction supervisor Thomas Lübke (in yellow hard hat) consults with workers on the ground floor.

Clockwise from top left:
Construction workers examine the rebar laid down in the chapel area before new concrete is poured.

A worker cleans out the building's cellar.

Wood subflooring awaits installation on the third floor.

During a weekly construction meeting, contractors discuss the condition of an old beam in the chapel area.

Top:
A worker installs the new wood subfloor on the second floor.

Bottom:
A worker digs through dirt and bones in the chapel area. Archaeologists believe the bones, like the dirt, were used as fill material when the building was built in 1564.

Top left:
Archaeologist Holger Rode shows a photo of skeletons discovered under the Old Latin School.

Bottom left:
The lead carpenter and the construction supervisor discuss the condition of floor joists in the building.

Top center:
Bernhard Naumann and Katja Köhler often assume the characters of Martin and Katie Luther for visitors to Wittenberg.

Bottom center:
A bust of Johannes Bugenhagen, Martin Luther's friend and pastor, graces the *Kirchplatz* where the Old Latin School is located.

Top right:
A bronze model of Wittenberg's old town on the city's marketplace includes the Old Latin School near the Town Church.

Bottom right:
Missionary and videographer Rick Steenbock shoots a video about Wittenberg with Rev. Mahsman.

Left:
The last of the graves excavated by archaeologists revealed an adult and four children—one, estimated to be a boy of 10, with a knife in his neck!

Below (top):
An archaeological worker gently removes dirt from a skeleton found among those under the present location of the building's elevator.

Below (bottom):
Archaeologists look for any sign of bones or graves in a ditch dug for plumbing under the first floor of the building.

Top left:
Graves discovered under the site of the elevator included one with an adult and four children.

Bottom left
These are the first skeletons discovered when workers excavated for the elevator shaft.

Bottom right:
Workers with the state archaeology office clean dirt away from the skeletons found under the location for the elevator.

Above:
A foggy morning in the Wittenberg *Altstadt* (old town).

Top right:
The north tower of the Town Church is visible from a skylight that was in the old roof of the Latin School. Dormer windows have replaced skylights in the top floor.

Bottom right:
The bronze statue of Martin Luther has stood on Wittenberg's market square since 1821.

Top left:
 Before construction could begin, sand was laid down to protect the cobblestones on the church plaza. Concrete was poured over the sand.

Top right:
 New wood timbers ready to be used.

Bottom left and center:
 Carpenters consult the plans, which indicated where the new wood would be "sistered" with the existing beams.

Right:
Rebar and concrete for the shaft of the building's elevator. The elevator shaft is especially strong because it is part of the building's support structure.

Bottom left:
LCMS President Matthew Harrison stands in a hole excavated to examine the structure of a load-bearing wall.

Bottom right:
Architect Katharina Gensicke discusses details of the *Kirchplatz* door with a restoration specialist.

Below:

Before actual renovation could begin, the floors and ceilings were torn out of the building. That led to the discovery that as much as 85 percent of the wood between the second and third floors had to be replaced because of rot or insect damage.

Top right:

Carpenters set aside still-sound pieces of beams from 1564 for possible use in making keepsakes of the building.

Bottom right:

Workers install steel reinforcements to old iron beams.

A prominent feature of the ground floor is the original 1564 pillar in the foyer. The pillar has been restored and will no doubt be a conversation piece as visitors gather in the building.

Far left, top and bottom:
It's a dirty job; workers remove flooring from the building's attic.

Immediate left:
The construction sign on the outside of the building shows how the school will look after renovation—when it was still thought it would be painted gray.

Below right:
Construction supervisor Thomas Lübke (in hat) listens to discussion of the condition of wood beams.

35

Clockwise, from top:
Extensive work was performed on the roof of the Old Latin School. After the old tiles were removed, the roof was covered in plastic.

A fungus was found in the west wall of the attic. The wall had to be destroyed and rebuilt.

Workers found rotten wood under the old roof.

Dr. Richard Carter of Concordia University St. Paul and his wife, Miriam, have a look at the attic during a visit to the building in March 2014.

Left column:
There was plenty of light in the attic after the roof tiles were removed in February 2014.

Below:
Scaffolding covered the entire building by February 2014.

Right column:
Carpenters check the plans for the new rafters. Roof tiles were replaced temporarily with plastic sheeting.

Below:
   A worker cleans old bricks for reuse.

Below:
   Architect Katharina Gensicke inspects a sample window built by joiners from *Tischlerei* Ludley (Ludley Carpentry).

Right column, top:
   Temporary supports hold things up as old ceilings and floors are torn out of the building.

Right column, bottom:
   Joiners install a sample window in the ground-floor foyer.

Left:
   ILSW Managing Director Rev. David Mahsman tells Concordia University students about plans for the Old Latin School.

Below:
A workman prepares to install a steel beam in the chapel.

Below:
Carpenters have a look at the iconic arched window in the east wall of the attic.

Right, top and bottom:
A steel stairway, installed in the early twentieth century but covered over for many decades, was revealed once again during demolition, then removed entirely.

Above:
Tearing out the old flooring revealed wood beams and joists that had been subject to rot and insect damage. Many had to be replaced.

Top left:
Architect Katharina Gensicke and construction supervisor Thomas Lübke (back to camera) give instructions to workmen.

Bottom left:
Construction sites aren't particularly safe to visit—especially when there are no floors!

Below:
An architect's rendering of how the Old Latin School was expected to look once renovations were complete.

Clockwise, from top left:

Considerable work went into preparing the form and rebar for the elevator shaft before the concrete was poured, floor by floor.

A researcher inspects stone steps in the building's cellar.

All the old stucco was removed from the outside of the building during renovation.

Old beams were sawed up and stored for possible later use.

This page:
Carpenters work to replace beams and floor joists. Some old wood was left, but reinforced with new wood.

Left:
An old iron pillar and iron beams still do the job on the ground floor.

Bottom left:
Efforts were made to protect the old stone stairs from the second floor to the third floor during construction.

Below:
The concrete elevator shaft extends into the attic.
Scaffolding, a contruction lift, and chutes to carry debris to a dumpster decorate the south side of the building during construction.

Top right:
A stonemason inspects the old sandstone window jambs. Most were repaired, but some had to be replaced.

Bottom right:
A bricklayer builds an interior sound-proofing wall.

Top left:
After the plaster was removed from the interior walls, repairs were made to the brickwork as necessary.

Bottom left:
In the chapel, a sixteenth-century beam is supported by a short section of a twenty-first-century beam.

Top center:
A stonemason repairs one of the sandstone window jambs.

Center:
Threaded tubing was used to pull together cracks in the brick walls.

Bottom center:
Bricks were laid in the heavy wooden framework to create a soundproofing wall in the dorm room area of the third floor.

Top right:
A number of construction signs decorate the east end of the building.

Bottom right:
Architect Katharina Gensicke consults her plans.

Top left:
Wood and steel crisscross above the chapel.

Bottom left:
Old iron bars that once covered the ground-floor windows have been removed.

Below, center:
Construction supervisor Thomas Lübke (in yellow hard hat) consults with carpenters regarding new wood floor joists.

Top right:
The Old Latin School sits near the Town Church (at left), which is also being renovated.

Bottom right:
The west wall of the attic was demolished for rebuilding. The terrace belongs to an adjacent building.

Richtfest

June 12, 2014, was a festival day at the Old Latin School. A traditional German *Richtfest* was celebrated to mark completion of the building's framework, to thank God and the workers for the progress to that point, and to ask the Lord's blessing on the building and the ministry that would take place there.

For the *Richtfest*, or "topping-out ceremony," a wreath with ribbons, called a *Richtkranz*, is raised onto the roof. The head carpenter recites a poem (the *Richtspruch*) in which he thanks the client for the work, wages, and bread and asks God's blessing upon the building. The *Richtfest* for the Old Latin School had good music, several speeches, and, of course, food and drink. The music was provided by wonderful musicians from Germany's Independent Evangelical-Lutheran Church (SELK); the speeches were offered by SELK Bishop Hans-Jörg Voigt, architect Helmut Keitel, and Wittenberg Lord Mayor Eckhard Naumann.

Representing the ILSW, I drove the last symbolic nail into the building frame (the "nail" was a foot-long spike!) and gave a speech.

Here is a little of what I said:

"Today we are celebrating a Richtfest, but I want you to know that our project is far more than this building. We are planning programs that will bring many students and other visitors to Wittenberg from other countries and from elsewhere in Germany, and we are planning programs that we hope will be of interest and benefit to the people of Wittenberg. Because there is so much more to our project than the building, there are many others for whom the board and I are grateful—many if not most of you are among them—but I will not take time now to mention everyone by name.

"I will not stop, though, without thanking the many donors in the U.S.A. and Germany who have contributed money for this project. They have given because they share our vision for a place of welcome in the heart of the Wittenberg Altstadt dedicated to Christian education and to the Gospel of Jesus Christ as proclaimed by Dr. Martin Luther and the other reformers. And of course, we thank God above all, without whose blessing none of this would happen."

Top right:
A carpenter prepares to take the *Richtkranz* onto the roof.

Bottom right:
The protective covering is pulled away from the open roof for the *Richtfest* ceremony.

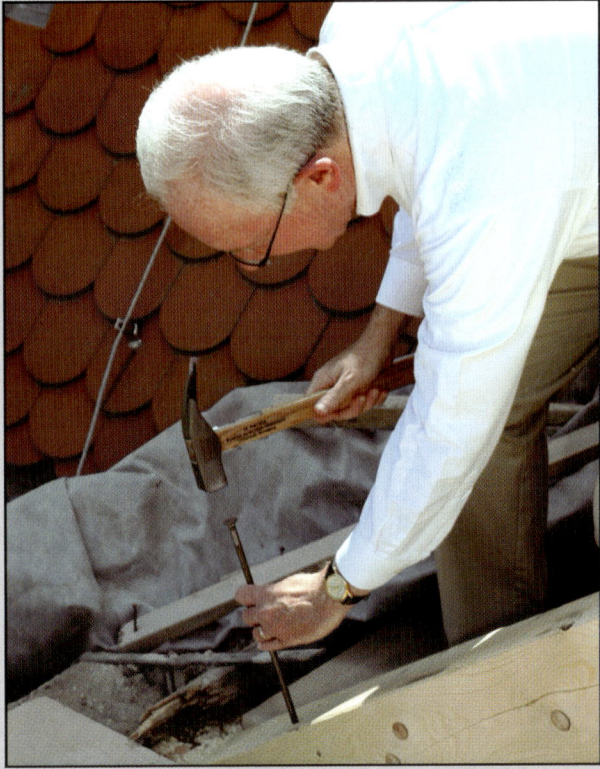

Clockwise from top left:
 The *Richtkranz* is secured to the roof.
 Wittenberg Lord Mayor Eckhard Naumann addresses the crowd.
 Rev. Mahsman drives the last symbolic nail into the building frame.
 Master Carpenter Kai Vater delivers the *Richtspruch* and makes a toast on the roof.

Left:
Brass musicians from SELK parishes, led by ILSW board Secretary Ulrich Schroeder, right, provided wonderful music for the celebration.

Right:
Guests and workers—the carpenters are in their traditional uniforms, complete with large black hats—listen to speeches on the ground floor of the building.

Right:
Guests listen to the speeches.

Far right:
SELK Bishop Hans-Jörg Voigt, left, visits with Superintendent Christian Beuchel of the Evangelical Church of Central Germany and with *Landrat* (county executive) Jürgen Dannenberg.

Right:
Guests and workers enjoying beer and brats in the cleaned up work area.

Far right:
Bishop Voigt speaks to guests at the *Richtfest*.

Renovations Continue

Left column, top to bottom:
   Construction of dormers in the attic significantly increases usable floor space there.
   The black plastic over the dormers protects the construction work from weather.
   Construction supervisor Thomas Lübke makes a point as he refers to construction plans for the dormers.

Middle column, top to bottom:
   The north front of the building, on Juedenstrasse, was not visible during most the renovation.
   Carpenters work on the south dormer in the attic.
   If at first it doesn't fit, try using a sledgehammer!

Below:
   A window on the ground floor, bricked in for many decades, is reopened.

Above, left to right:
    The small sculpture of an infant with a skull that graces the *Kirchplatz* doorway to the building is symbolic of the transience of human life.
    Pipes were installed to carry hot water to the radiators throughout the building.
    New windows had to be made and installed. The window hardware would come later.
    Occasionally, a brick with a pattern would be uncovered. The pattern, such as this one, told the brick makers that it was the last brick made the previous day.

Right:
    Architect Katharina Gensicke and *Tischler* (joiner or cabinetmaker) Dirk Ludley go over plans for windows in the building.

Far right:
    A soundproofing wall of brick goes up between the faculty apartment and a student dorm room.
(Those professors can be noisy!)

Below:
Plastering the walls. One person sprays plaster on the wall while another smoothes it out.

Below:
This sandstone placard on the Juedenstrasse side of the building takes note of the renovation and expansion of the Old Latin School (or "Wittenberg Gymnasium") in 1828.

Below:
Stucco was removed from the sandstone window jambs, which were painted but otherwise left natural, as they were when the building was first built.

Middle column and bottom left:
   Workers install and inspect new tiles on the roof.

Below, top:
   This shot, taken September 18, 2014, shows the south-side roof tiles and dormer in progress and the bare brick under the scaffolding.

Below, top to bottom:
   Looking east out the emergency exit in the attic offers a view of the Town Church and the Bugenhagenhaus, the former parsonage.
   A tower of the Town Church stands over the roof of the Old Latin School.

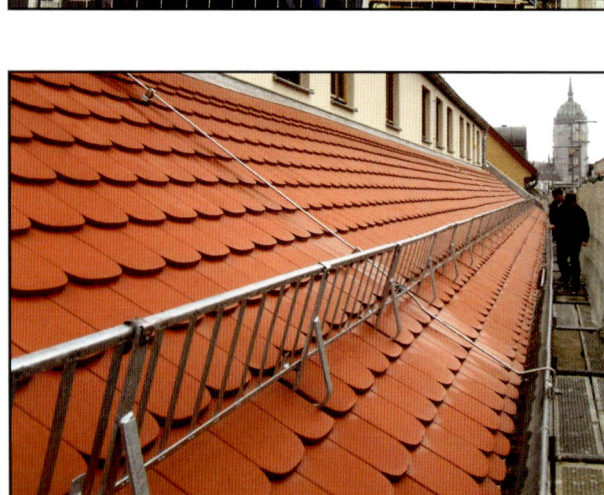

Below, top to bottom:

The chapel ceiling features two wood beams from the sixteenth century. The green beam shown here still is visible and has been restored.

A new sandstone window jamb is delivered for installation on the north side of the building.

Drywall installers use a laser level.

Below, top to bottom:

This window is larger than the other attic windows because it is an emergency exit.

The chapel window that was once bricked in sports one of the few old window frames in the building. It was moved from another location to the "new" window opening.

Below, top to bottom:

Plumbing and drywall appear on the ceiling of the foyer on the ground floor. The pipes later would be covered.

Workers install new insulation.

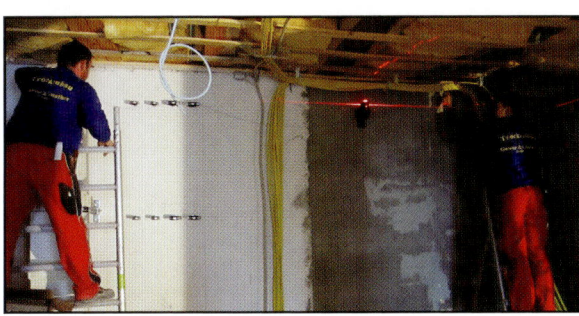

Below, top to bottom:
   Painting is largely done on the south side of the building. The scaffolding is still up, but not for long.

   Hartmut Rademann's models illustrate various possibilities for the corpus—the body of Christ—on the chapel crucifix.

Below, top to bottom:
   Wiring snakes around the top floor.

   Workers put the finishing touches on new stucco for the east side of the building.

   A painter applies fire-retardant paint to one of the steel pillars in the chapel.

Below, top to bottom:
   Tablets are more convenient than paper floor plans.

   By Reformation weekend in October 2014, painting had been done on the south side of the building and the scaffolding removed. The east side of the building would be finished next.

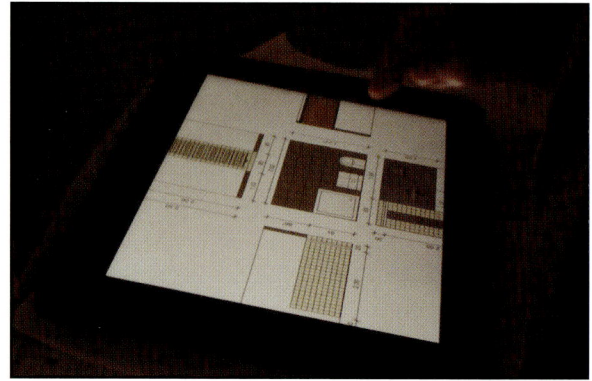

Below, top to bottom:

Some sections of the sandstone window jambs had to be replaced with new stone. An example is the right-side vertical jamb on this window.

The *Kirchplatz* portal and the stone inscription over it were not restored when the rest of the south front of the building was renovated. Restoration waited until March 2015 and was one of the last pieces of the renovation to be completed.

Below:

Restaurator (restorer) Sven Raecke works on the sandstone plaque that was placed on the Juedenstrasse (north) side of the building when it was renovated and expanded in 1828.

Below, bottom right:

Although not really part of the Old Latin School, a portion of the gold-colored building next door appears visually to be part of our building. In a separate project, workmen also renovated the exterior of that building to give a clean look to the whole.

Below and bottom right:
Gas and water lines snake out of a ground-floor service room . . . and down the hallway.

Below, top:
The old beam and pillar are a contrast to the new plumbing in the foyer.

Above:
This is all the equipment necessary to provide hot-water heat for the entire Old Latin School. Two small furnaces are on the left.

Below, top to bottom:
　A new radiator and windowsill find their places under a dorm-room window that faces the Town Church.

　The 1564 pillar in the foyer was wrapped in plastic to protect it when the walls were being plastered.

Below, top to bottom:
　A worker installs cables in the group room kitchen.

　Radiators are connected to hot-water pipes, which lie under the floor in the bookstore, foyer, and chapel.

　Dry-screed pellets form a smooth surface under the dorm-room floors.

Below, top to bottom:
　Walls begin to take shape around the living area in the attic apartment. This is looking to the north, toward the kitchen area.

　Wiring and plumbing await connection in the ground-floor service room.

Below:

June Johnson, an English expat who lives in Wittenberg, took this picture of the Old Latin School on November 12, 2014, from her balcony east of the building and across Juedenstrasse.

Bottom center:

With painting done on the north side of the building, the scaffolding was removed. Note that the nearest two columns of windows actually belong to the gold-colored bank building next door, even though visually they appear to be part of the Old Latin School. The bank renovated the exterior of that part of its building at the same time as the north side of the school was renovated.

Below, top and bottom:

After painting was done on the east end of the school building, the local electric company (Stadtwerke Lutherstadt Wittenberg) reinstalled the decorative streetlight that had been attached before renovation began.

Left column, top to bottom:

The north-south hallway on the ground floor is flanked by new frames for glass fire doors and walls.

This is the view of the chapel from the raised chancel, from the north end of the room to the south.

The foyer takes shape in this view to the west from the chapel door.

Middle column, top to bottom:

Looking from the hallway toward the chapel gives another view of work on the foyer.

Workers from *Tischlerei* Ludley (Ludley Joinery) remove an inner door from the exit to the church plaza. The Ludley firm made the doors and windows for the renovated school.

Far right, top:

The floor of the chancel in the chapel is slightly higher than the rest of the room.

Below, top to bottom:
  After delivery of the Otis elevator, the base and other parts are stored in the future bookstore to await installation.

  Installation of the elevator in the shaft began in January 2015 and took several weeks.

Below, top to bottom:
  Workers at the top of the shaft stand three stories above . . .

  . . . the workers at the bottom during installation of the elevator.

Below, top:
  Here's the view down the elevator shaft from the top floor during installation.

Left, bottom:
  Today's elevators demand today's electronics.

Right, bottom:
  A workman from Otis adjusts the elevator doors on the ground floor.

Below, top to bottom:

Of course, the top of the elevator normally would not be visible, but here it is during the testing phase of its installation.

An independent, certified testing agency spent most of a day assuring the safe operation of the elevator. Tests included placing weights in the car. Each of these carts weighs 200 kilos (441 pounds).

Below, top to bottom:

The regional service manager from Otis Elevator explains emergency operation of the elevator. In the background is Christian Eggert, managing director of nearby *Colleg Wittenberg*, which is working with the ILSW on lodging in the Old Latin School.

The floor of the elevator is the same slate tile used on the ground floor of the building.

Below, top to bottom:

A welder replaces the railing that had been removed around a drainage canal to allow scaffolding to be erected on the north side of the school.

Once the railing was replaced, the small drainage canal that runs along the north side of the Old Latin School was uncovered.

Left top to bottom:

The year construction originally began on the Old Latin School—1564—is chiseled into the stone plaque over the *Kirchplatz* door into the building.

Floor covering in *Dachgeschoss* (attic) apartment.

Right column top:

The foyer continues to take shape . . . and stores materials for use elsewhere on the ground floor.

Right column middle:

A modern stonemason works with power tools and plenty of ear and respiratory protection.

Right column, very bottom:

Paint and plaster were removed from portions of the stairway walls from the second to third floors, and they will stay unpainted to reveal their historic look.

Above (middle column):

Patches of test paint were applied to a beam and the pillar from 1564 for inspection by state historic-preservation authorities. The authorities agreed with a gray paint for the beam but directed that the pillar be painted in a cream color.

Below, top to bottom:

The doorways are prepared in the faculty apartment.

This historic door, found resting against a wall in the poor condition shown here, has been restored and installed in the faculty apartment (see next page).

Below, top to bottom:

A painter paints the ceiling in the large apartment on the top floor.

The poor condition of the old stone steps from the ground floor to the second floor was revealed after the linoleum covering them was removed.

Below, top to bottom:

Acoustician Manfred Weisse, holding the microphone, tests the sound quality of the chapel. He made a number of recommendations for improving the acoustics in the chapel.

Restoration of the 1564 column included carefully placing wood into the larger cracks—visible as the light line running up the length of the pillar—and a steel collar around the top of it.

Below, top to bottom:
One of the small, but important, details is installation of emergency exit signs.

As work progressed on the third floor, lights were installed and the hallway was taped, ready for final painting.

Below, top to bottom:
A platform was erected in the stairwell between the third and second floors to allow access to the windows.

The drop-down ladder on the top floor provides access to a crawl space and part of the building's ventilation system.

Below, top to bottom:
The main power-supply closet is on the ground floor.

Each dorm room has its own bathroom. Tiling and fixtures had been installed, but the shower enclosure and other details remained to be done when this photo taken.

Two historic doors found in the building when construction began have been restored and installed in the second-floor faculty apartment.

Below, top to bottom:

A tile installer puts finishing touches on the area of the chapel in which the baptismal font will be placed.

Electricians hold up a sample ceiling light for the chapel.

After the elevator was placed into operation, particle board protection was installed so that it could be used to transport workers and materials to the upper floors. The stairwell was closed so that the steps could be renovated.

Below, top to bottom:

Wood parquet flooring is stacked in the foyer to await installation in the chapel.

A painter prepares the chapel ceiling for painting.

The bedroom in the third-floor faculty apartment was the first room in the building to get the final coat of paint on the walls.

Below, top to bottom:

Patches of a ninteenth-century wall decoration are preserved near the ceiling in one of the second-floor dormitory rooms.

After the walls were painted in the faculty-apartment living room and kitchen areas, the wood-grained flooring was laid.

Below, top to bottom:

The living-room area in the attic apartment features exposed wood beams and posts. The beams and posts on the left are new; those on the right are original to 1828, when the building was renovated and enlarged.

Doors are stacked in the foyer to await installation in the dormitory rooms and elsewhere.

Below (series):

Throughout most of construction, the church-plaza cobblestones and possible graves under them were protected from the weight of construction vehicles by a thick layer of sand topped by concrete. By the end of February, the heavy vehicles were gone, and workers set about removing the concrete and sand.

Above:

The doorway on the Juedenstrasse side of the building was boarded up for several weeks while the door was renovated by the *Tischler* (joiner or cabinetmaker) who also made the new windows and other wooden features for the building.

Below, top to bottom:

A worker installs the wood-parquet floor in the chapel.

New slate-tiled steps ascend to the top floor.

Below, top to bottom:

Two historic doors were restored, with new hardware that replicates that of the era (top and middle).

The chapel floor stands finished and awaits the arrival of furnishings. Those include the baptismal font, which will be placed inside the slate-tiled circle at right.

Below:

The sandstone steps from the second floor to the third floor are repaired. (The steps from the ground floor to the second floor had to be replaced with new sandstone.)

Below, top to bottom:

Only the two offices on the fourth floor are carpeted. Dormers provide more floor space, but wood beams remain.

Every dormitory room has its own bathroom with shower.

Below:

In the top two photos, a workman digs a ditch to connect the building to the city sewer system. Fortunately, no graves were uncovered in the process!

In the bottom photo, staff from the architect's office and joiner Dirk Ludley make a final inspection of the windows made by Ludley and his skilled carpenters.

Below:

Attractive pendulum light fixtures are installed in the foyer.

Below, top to bottom:

Stonemasons' tools sit on the sandstone steps.

Staff from *Tischlerei* Ludley (Ludley carpentry) install the newly restored doors at the Juedenstrasse entrance.

Below, top to bottom:

Here's a first look at the repaired sandstone steps between the second and third floors.

These restored doors lead to Juedenstrasse. The colored glass above the doors was also restored.

Below, top to bottom:

The water works!

The *Kirchplatz* entrance got new doors, which replicated the originals.

Below, top to bottom:
  New lights grace the bookstore.
  A restoration specialist works on nineteenth-century wall designs discovered in the stairway between the second and third floors.
  A new light hangs in the chapel.

Top right:
  This dramatic photo of the Old Latin School and the Town Church, St. Mary's, was taken by June Johnson from her balcony across the street.

Bottom center:
  The lights work in the foyer!

Bottom right:
  LED light strips warn of a small step up.

Top left:
A plasterer renovates the vaulted ceiling over the Juedenstrasse entrance.

Bottom left:
Wooden rings are installed at the bottom of the steel pillars in the chapel to give a more finished look.

Center, top and bottom:
A stone doorway was repaired and moved to the entrance of the kitchen in the group room for use by guests staying in the building.

Below:
Wall designs from the nineteenth century, discovered under layers of paint, are restored in the stairway from the second to the third floor.

Restoration specialists painstakingly restore the iconic portal, coats of arms, and sandstone plaque at the *Kirchplatz* entrance to the Old Latin School. The colors of the coats of arms—of the Saxon prince elector and of the city of Wittenberg—were determined in an inspection already made in 2009.

Renovation Surprises

Structural engineer Thomas Lübke had some sleepless nights early in the renovation of the Old Latin School. He was worried about how to keep the building from falling down.

What kept him awake was the discovery that perhaps 85 percent of the wooden beams and floor joists between the second and third floors were so insect-damaged and rotten—probably from water leakage when the building was renovated and expanded back in 1828—that they had to be replaced. How do you take out such a large part of the structure without it collapsing? Very carefully.

"He was near to a nervous breakdown," laughs architect Helmut Keitel, the head of *bc Architekten + Ingenieure*, the firm that planned and supervised the recent work at the Old Latin School. (The "bc" stands for *Bau*, or Construction, Consult.)

But the problem was solved, the wood was replaced, the building is still standing, and Lübke can sleep again.

Shortly before the renovation was completed at the end of March 2015, I talked with Lübke, Keitel, and architect Katharina Gensicke. (The three spoke in German, so their quotes are translations.)

"We have a lot of experience with [old] buildings," Keitel said. "But there are always surprises." The rotten wood was one surprise, and not a pleasant one. But the biggest surprise, Keitel said, was when state archaeologists found skeletons at the bottom of the elevator shaft.

Whenever digging was done in the building, archaeologists from the federal state of Saxony-Anhalt, where Lutherstadt Wittenberg is located, were on site just in case something interesting would be uncovered.

During excavation for the elevator-shaft footings, some skeletons were discovered. These obviously had been graves in the churchyard of the *Stadtkirche*, or Town Church.

All work on the elevator shaft, as well as some other construction work, came to a stop. After six weeks of digging, the archaeologists had removed twenty-two skeletons, all stacked in layers on top of one another in the space of a small elevator. The last skeletons to be removed were in a grouping of five—one adult and four children. One of the children, estimated to be a 10-year-old boy, still had a knife blade in his neck!

The archaeologists had no idea what had happened to these people. They estimated that the skeletons were from the thirteenth century. If so, they had been there some 300 years before the Old Latin School was even built. All the skeletons were taken to the State Museum of PreHistory in Halle, where they are being studied. We hope one day to have a report and more information about this particular "surprise."

> "We have a lot of experience with [old] buildings... but there are always surprises."

From the start of construction in October 2013 until its completion at the very end of March 2015, I attended weekly *Bauberatungen*, construction-consultation meetings, generally led by Lübke and attended by whatever contractors were working on the building at the moment. It was not unusual for a problem to crop up that had to be solved. That's the thing with such an old building.

Actually, the Old Latin School is not simply an old building that presented construction problems to be solved. It's also a historic building. It is protected under German law. So, not only did we deal with the various construction and safety authorities, but also with the historic-preservation authorities—the *Landesamt für Denkmalpflege und Archäologie* (State Office for Historic Preservation and Archaeology).

Often referred to simply as *Denkmalpflege* or *Denkmalschutz* (monument protection), these officials had the final say for many features of our historic building. They either decided or approved the paint colors inside and outside. They required new or repaired sandstone steps from the ground floor to the third floor. They directed that 450-year-old wooden beams on the ground floor be preserved, which meant installing steel pillars that block some sight lines in the chapel instead of the pillar-free steel-beam construction that had been planned.

> The building has a past, and it now has a future.

While the need for the steel pillars may be unfortunate, we happily complied with the directives in most cases. Good examples are preservation of the original wood pillar in the foyer and the colorful restoration of the sandstone plaque and coats of arms over the *Kirchplatz* doorway. These, in fact, already have become recognized "trademarks" of the Old Latin School.

One historic feature of the building that was not originally on the *Denkmalschutz* radar was the way the walls of the stairwell from the second floor to the third floor were painted in the nineteenth century. The nineteenth-century paint was discovered during investigations ordered by Jens-Uwe Anwand of Dresden, who was the architect for an earlier renovation plan.

"The *Denkmalschutz* is happy [Anwand] found the painting," said Gensicke. "It's a window to the past."

The building has a past, and it now has a future. Architect Gensicke said it like this: "I think it's a very good project because it was financed by the church and private people when it was built [in 1564] to bring education to kids. Now, after hundreds of years, it goes back to being for education—and even for Lutheran education."

And, we would add, for proclamation of the Gospel.

Top row (left to right):

Architect Katharina Gensicke inspects installation of one of the building's glass fire doors.

Handrails and protective metal work await painting in the stairwell.

A handicap-accessible restroom is available on the ground floor.

Bottom row (left to right):

The door to the chapel incorporates a cross design.

A small platform is the emergency exit for the top floor of the building.

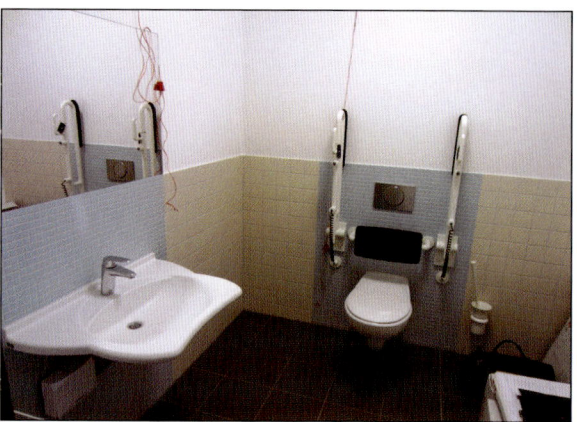

Top row (left to right):
Finishing touches include final painting around the chapel doorway and sandstone paint on the doorway to the group-room kitchen and on a pillar between the windows in the bookstore.

Bottom left:
New fixtures, including track lights, illuminate the bookstore.

Bottom middle and right:
Early one morning, this truck delivered the cabinets and major appliances for the building's three kitchens, two tea kitchens, and sacristy.

Below:
   Books donated by Concordia Publishing House await unpacking and their new (and hopefully temporary) home on the bookstore shelves.

Below, top to bottom:
   Here are two early shots of the group-room kitchen, which guests can use to store and prepare food for meals or snacks.

   Shelving in the housekeeping room on the top floor now holds towels, sheets, and cleaning supplies.

Below, top to bottom:
   This tea kitchen on the ground floor will help with receptions and other gatherings in the foyer.

   The faculty apartment on the third floor also has its own kitchen.

Below, top to bottom:

Delivering a solid sandstone altar takes experience and the proper equipment.

Workers take care to place the altar very precisely. Once it's in place, it won't be going anywhere. (Photos courtesy David Bueltmann)

Below, top and middle:

The checkout desk in the bookstore includes a glass display case for smaller items.

The sandstone altar was designed by artist and woodcarver Hartmut Rademann to reflect the arched *Kirchplatz* entrance door to the Old Latin School.

Below:

Former Central Illinois District President and organist David Bueltmann, who volunteered for more than a month in the Old Latin School before the dedication, tries out the new organ. The small organ was built for the chapel by Henk Klop Early Keyboard Instruments in the Netherlands. (This photo was taken with Bueltmann's smartphone by Henk Klop's son, who delivered the organ.)

Left:

The baptismal font was crafted from the same sandstone as the altar.

Below:

The chapel space was fairly empty until the altar, font, ambo, organ, and chairs arrived.

Dedication

Many prayers were said in the weeks, months, and even years leading up to dedication day for the Old Latin School. And many more were said that day, Sunday, May 3, 2015.

The final prayer of the formal dedication ceremony was offered by LCMS President Matthew Harrison: "Almighty God, heavenly Father, without whom no word or work of ours avails, grant Your blessing to all who use this guest house and educational facility. Help them grow day by day in the knowledge of Your will and in the grace to perform it, to the honor and praise of Your name and the good of all people. . . ."

I firmly believe those words, that without God's blessing, none of our words or works avail anything. But with His blessing and by His grace, even our poor and inadequate efforts can bring forth something remarkable.

Most of the actual renovation of the Old Latin School, the *Alte Lateinschule*, was finished a month ahead of the dedication. But April still saw the installation of three complete kitchens—in two apartments and the group room—as well as two tea kitchens and a sacristy; bookstore shelving and fixtures; library bookcases; and window treatments. Furniture was delivered and assembled throughout the building. The Internet server and telephone lines were connected to the outside world. So many things to do to get ready.

But it's unavoidable—a set day will come, ready or not.

In the case of the Old Latin School, it was more of a set weekend, a weekend of celebrating. The Sunday-afternoon dedication worship service and ceremony were sandwiched between a Saturday-night concert for the Wittenberg community and a Sunday-evening reception, followed by another concert.

Guests came from all over the world, thanks in large part to a theological conference hosted by the Missouri Synod's Commission on Theology and Church Relations and the Office of the President that began with the weekend's festivities. Some 450 guests were reported in the *Stadtkirche*, St. Mary's, for the festival worship that kicked off the actual dedication.

Martin Luther preached more than 2,000 sermons in this historic church, which is just steps from the Old Latin School. On May 3, it was President Harrison who mounted the pulpit and proclaimed Law and Gospel to those gathered in the church. He reminded his listeners of the last words Luther wrote, found on a piece of paper in his pocket after he died: "We are beggars, this is true." We contribute nothing to our salvation; we only receive God's gifts in Jesus Christ.

Others who led the project to this point also had roles in the service. Bishop Hans-Jörg Voigt of Germany's *Selbständige Evangelisch-Lutherische Kirche* (SELK), the Independent Evangelical-Lutheran Church, was the litur-

gist. The eight lectors—all of them connected to the project or its history—included Dr. Bruce G. Kintz, president and CEO of Concordia Publishing House, and Rev. Dr. Michael Kumm, chairman of the Board of Directors of the LCMS and of the International Lutheran Society of Wittenberg.

Immediately following the service, the officiating clergy and worshipers moved to the now-familiar church-plaza door of the Old Latin School for the dedication ceremony itself.

Just outside the door, there was one of those glitches that can happen no matter how much planning is done. As architect Helmut Keitel walked to the door for the ceremonial *Schlüsselübergabe* (handing over of the keys), he motioned to me that he actually had no keys, probably because he had just arrived back in Germany that morning after a trip to the United States. So I hiked up my alb—because I was

Left page:
　Despite my serious expression, I was pleased to carry the processional cross and lead the officiating clergy into (and, later, out of) the festival service in the historic Town Church, St. Mary's, for the dedication of the Old Latin School.

This page:
　Many of those who traveled to Wittenberg for the dedication and for a theological conference that followed it worshiped in English on Sunday morning (May 3). The service was held in the auditorium at the Leucorea, the former Wittenberg University buildings.

　Ulrich Schroeder and Dr. Bruce G. Kintz, two members of the International Lutheran Society of Wittenberg Supervisory Board, sing one of the hymns during the dedication service.

　Missionary Rev. Dr. Christopher Ahlman was organist for the dedication service.

the crucifer, I was vested and standing by the door—and fished my own keys from my pants pocket. I quickly handed them to Keitel, who in turn gave them to Kintz, who represented the ILSW, owners of the building. I guess it really didn't matter that the key ring held a half dozen keys, including my car key—the door was already unlocked.

Once inside, the officiating clergy and about 60 of the guests moved to the chapel. Because there were more guests than room inside, many stood outside listening over loudspeakers. We were blessed with good weather.

Inside, we separately dedicated and asked God's blessing on the baptismal font, altar, pulpit, cross, and organ before President Harrison gave that final prayer for the entire building.

Back outside, Dr. Reiner Haseloff, *Ministerpräsident* (governor) of Saxony-Anhalt, the federal state in which Wittenberg is located, and Propst (Regional Bishop) Siegfried Kasparick, of the Evangelical Church of Central Germany, brought greetings. Kasparick also brought greetings on behalf of the city and Lord Mayor-elect Torsten Zugehör, who had fallen ill that morning.

"We are faced with a complex yet exciting situation here in this area of Germany," Kasparick said, speaking first in English. "On the one hand, visiting the Luther sites is of great national and international interest. . . . On the other hand, many people have no idea of God. Already we have the third generation (of East Germans) for whom faith plays no role whatsoever. The church is foreign to them."

Kasparick noted that 85 percent of Wittenbergers belong to no church at all. "Yet, since the Wall came down, we can make out a new development: Most people are not antichurch. They are interested in church programs," he said. This is encouraging information.

While many well-meaning well-wishers have talked as though the work is now done, it's really just beginning. The Old Latin School is not an end in itself, but rather a means to an end. It is to be a place for Christian education, for strengthening the faith and mission awareness of believers. And it's also to be a place for Gos-

Above:
Rev. Dr. Wilhelm Torgerson, first director of the ILSW, gave a hand-painted icon depicting Martin Luther to the Old Latin School on the occasion of its dedication.

pel outreach to those who do not yet know or believe in Jesus Christ.

We want this to be a place from which God's gracious gifts in Christ are freely given to beggars like us and to the many thousands of people with whom we will come into contact.

Left column, top to bottom:
   The recent renovation of the Town Church, the "Mother Church of the Reformation," made it an even more wonderful venue for the dedication worship service.
   Rev. Dr. Michael Kumm, chairman of the ILSW Supervisory Board, reads one of the lessons during the dedication service.
   CPH President and CEO Dr. Bruce G. Kintz was a lector for the dedication service.

Middle, top to bottom:
   LCMS President Rev. Dr. Matthew Harrison preached the dedication sermon. He reflected in part on Martin Luther's final sermon in the same church, in which Luther urged his listeners to have a simple, childlike faith.
   SELK Bishop Hans-Jörg Voigt and LCMS President Matthew Harrison jointly pronounce the benediction at the close of the dedication service.

Below:
   Dedication Day, May 3, concluded with a concert of Reformation-era music in the Town Church.

Top photo and directly below:
  Worshipers who had been in the Town Church for the festival worship service stand outside the Old Latin School door for the dedication ceremony that followed.
  During the dedication ceremony, Rev. Mahsman blesses the ambo—it will serve as a pulpit—in the chapel. The baptismal font, altar, cross, and organ also were blessed individually by officiating pastors.

Bottom right two photos:
  A brass choir provided music outside the church prior to the dedication service, as well as after the service and before the dedication ceremony at the Old Latin School.
  LCMS President Matthew Harrison concluded the dedication ceremony by asking God's blessing on the entire Old Latin School building.

Right:
  Not only was the organ blessed, but missionary Christopher Ahlman also played a short piece.

Below, top to bottom:

Worship leaders and worshipers sing a hymn outside the Old Latin School door at the beginning of the dedication ceremony. The ceremony at the school followed the dedication worship service in the Town Church.

As part of the ceremony, architect Helmut Keitel gives the key for the Old Latin School to Dr. Bruce G. Kintz, a member of the ILSW Supervisory Board.

Below:

LCMS President Matthew Harrison greets Saxony-Anhalt *Minister-präsident* (governor) Reiner Haseloff, left, and *Propst* Siegfried Kasparick of the Protestant Church of Central Germany following the dedication ceremony. Haseloff and Kasparick brought greetings to the dedication assembly. In the background is Rev. Dr. Jon Vieker, senior assistant to Harrison.

Below:

Rev. Dr. Albert B. Collver III, LCMS director of church relations and assistant to the president, blessed the baptismal font in the chapel.

Far Below: (group photo)

The Concordia Publishing House Board of Directors with Jonathan Schultz, VP and Corporate Counsel (in red tie); next to Dr. Bruce G. Kintz, President and CEO; and Rev. Paul McCain, Publisher and Executive Director of Editorial (directly behind Dr. Kintz).

Top left:
The crucifix for the chapel was hand-carved by Hartmut Rademann, a master carver in the *Erzgebirge* (Ore Mountains) of eastern Germany.

Below:
Worship leaders sing a hymn at the Old Latin School door at the beginning of the dedication ceremony.

Below:
Music—including music played on period instruments—had a large role in the weekend of dedication festivities.

Above:
Bishop Hans-Jörg Voigt of Germany's Independent Evangelical-Lutheran Church addresses guests at a reception that followed the dedication worship service and ceremony.

Left:
Two presidents—Rev. Dr. Matthew C. Harrison of the LCMS and Dr. Bruce G. Kintz of CPH—share a light moment during the dedication festivities May 3, 2015.

Below, top to bottom:

CPH President and CEO Dr. Bruce G. Kintz visits the Old Latin School bookstore during the dedication weekend.

The bookstore features books from CPH and from German publishers.

The chapel is now furnished.

Below:

The foyer is just outside the chapel, featuring the restored 1564 pillar.

Middle:

Another chapel view with its altar and crucifix.

Below (series):

Below are the baptismal font and two views of the chapel.

Below, top to bottom:
The school includes a group room for guests and two offices.

Middle, top to bottom:
The faculty apartment has a living area and separate bedroom.
At bottom is a typical dorm room.

Right column:
Here are the ground floor hallway (top) and the staircase (middle) from the third floor down to the second, featuring the historic 19th century wall decorations.
The Old Latin School is now an attractive feature of Wittenberg's historic center.

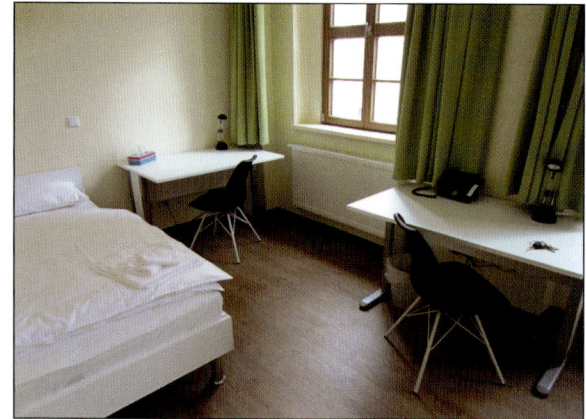

For who would believe that the church at Wittenberg, Kemberg, and other places where Baptism and the Word are, is in God's eyes an ivory palace?

Yet it actually is.

For Baptism is not something inane; neither is the Word, nor the government of the church; nor is the comfort of the downtrodden something meaningless. If you wish to judge by external appearances, what do you see here at Wittenberg of value? You see nothing splendid about the church; the city is actually built of clay, and yet it is an ivory palace of Christ. So even the poorest village in which there is a pastor and some believers is a palace of ivory. But in order to see this, you need other than physical eyes. Its value cannot be determined by appearance, by the judgment of the five senses or reason, nor by laws, nor by the arts or philosophy; but according to God's Word—by the fact that the Word is there, Baptism, the Eucharist, divine governance, the consolation of consciences, the fear of God, trust in God, waiting upon God, the imitation of Christ, and the like. You should look around for these things, and when you see them somewhere, do not let external appearance or anything else influence you, but simply conclude: "Here is Christ in palaces of ivory; here Christ dwells. Though this kingdom is nothing in appearance, it is nevertheless most delightful in God's eyes."

—Psalm 45 (1533–34), *Luther's Works* 12:255

Conference on Confessional Leadership

On May 3–8, 2015, confessional church leaders from around the world gathered in Wittenberg to discuss global challenges and opportunities under the theme "Celebrating the Reformation Rightly: Remembrance, Repentance, Rejoicing."

"Here we are in 'Little Wittenberg,' where it all began almost 500 years ago. We are here to celebrate the Reformation rightly: to remember, to repent, and to rejoice. The future of world Lutheranism truly is in the balance nearly 500 years after Luther shook the church and the world by posting his theses on the door of the Castle Church, just across town."
—Joel Lehenbauer, Executive Director, Commission on Theology and Church Relations

Top right:
Bishop Hans-Jörg Voigt of the Independent Evangelical Lutheran Church (SELK) welcomes church leaders Tuesday, May 5, 2015, at the International Conference on Confessional Leadership in the 21st Century in Wittenberg, Germany.

Bottom right:
Group photograph of the International Conference on Confessional Leadership in the 21st Century at the Town and Parish Church of St. Mary's on Wednesday, May 6, 2015, in Wittenberg, Germany.

Below, top to bottom:
Rev. Dr. Lawrence R. Rast Jr., president of Concordia Theological Seminary in Fort Wayne, Ind., shakes hands with Rev. Dr. Joel Lehenbauer, executive director of the LCMS Commission on Theology and Church Relations.

Rev. Dr. Matthew C. Harrison addresses church leaders.

Below and top right:
Church leaders listen and take notes Tuesday, May 5, 2015, at the International Conference on Confessional Leadership in the 21st Century in Wittenberg, Germany.

Bottom right:
Rev. Dr. Robert Kolb, International Research Emeritus Professor for the Institute for Mission Studies at Concordia Seminary, St. Louis, addresses the gathering.

Below, top to bottom:
Church leaders listen to presentations.

Below, top to bottom:
Worshipers gather for Matins at the Town and Parish Church of St. Mary's during the International Conference on Confessional Leadership in the 21st Century.

Below:
Rev. Dr. Timothy Quill, dean of International Studies and associate professor of Pastoral Ministry and Mission for Concordia Theological Seminary, Fort Wayne, Ind., leads Matins.

Below, top to bottom:
Lutheran church leaders gather at the Town and Parish Church of St. Mary's for Matins.

Below, top to bottom:
Rev. Dr. Albert C. Collver discusses architecture with fellow church leaders.

Rev. Dr. Matthew C. Harrison (center) leads a tour.

Church leaders listen and observe during a tour of Wittenberg.

Below:
The tour passes by the Martin Luther statue in Wittenberg.

Below, top to bottom:
Rev. Harrison leads the tour group to the Old Latin School. The bottom picture shows them gathered in the chapel.

Middle column, bottom image:
Artwork at the top of the replica door of the Castle Church.

The coats of arms of Johann Bugenhagen, Martin Luther and Philipp Melanchthon.

Below:
The Executive Committee of the International Lutheran Council meets in the newly renovated Old Latin School.

Below, top to bottom:
The Rev. Roland Gustafsson, the bishop presiding over the work of The Mission Province in Sweden, gives a presentation.

Attendees listen to Bishop Emmanuel Makala of the Evangelical Lutheran Church in Tanzania—South-East of Lake Victoria Diocese.

Below:
Church leaders listen and take notes during the conference.

Almighty God, heavenly Father, without whom no word or work of ours avails, grant Your blessing to all who use this guesthouse and educational facility. Help them grow day by day in the knowledge of Your will and in the grace to perform it, to the honor and praise of Your name and the good of all people. Amen.

—Rev. Dr. Matthew C. Harrison

Prayer offered at the dedication ceremony

of the Old Latin School,

Sunday, May 3, 2015

Celebrate The Wittenberg Project with the official commemorative medallion

The Wittenberg Project medallion is all about history in the making.

A great conversation starter, this three-inch medallion with antique bronze finish features the Old Latin School on the front —a historic site in the heart of Wittenberg, Germany. The back displays Luther's Rose and the message "Sola Gratia, Sola Fide, Sola Scriptura."

Your medallion comes custom fitted in a cherry wood case. Order this piece of history today, a must-have Lutheran collector's item for your desk or bookshelf!

For more information and to order, visit **cph.org/wittenbergmedallion**

Back View